SHADOW AND THE COCONUT CAPER

Written by Richard Hays

Illustrated by Chris Sharp

A Faith Parenting Guide can be found on page 3.

Faith Kids®
is an imprint of Cook Communications Ministries,
Colorado Springs, Colorado 80918
Cook Communications, Paris, Ontario
Kingsway Communications, Eastbourne, England

SHADOW AND THE COCONUT CAPER
©2001 by The Illustrated Word, Inc.

First printing, 2001
Printed in Canada
05 04 03 02 01   5 4 3 2 1

Digital art and design: Gary Currant
Executive Producer: Kenneth R. Wilcox

Faith Parenting Guide

Shadow and the Coconut Caper

Life issue: My children are learning to treat others as they want to be treated.

Sight: Find the Golden Rule in the Bible (Matthew 7:12). Memorize it with your children.

Sound: Show your children the difference between words that express the Golden Rule and words that don't. Change roles with your children—you be the child, and let them take turns being the parent. Have them ask you to do a specific chore, such as cleaning your room. Respond negatively first: "No way! I'm having too much fun playing!" Then have them ask you again. Answer them kindly and obediently: "Sure, Mom. I'll get right on it." Talk about how your responses made them feel.

Touch: Have your children draw pictures demonstrating the Golden Rule. Hang them in prominent places to remind you and your family of God's plan for how we are to treat each other..

One bright morning Shadow the raccoon cheerfully skipped through Noah's Park with a basket filled with coconuts. When he came to Screech's Hollow, he ran to the tree house where Screech the monkey lived and he carefully carved an arrow into the dirt. Then he dropped a coconut on top of it. "This will get that little monkey!" he smirked, and skipped away.

Shadow disappeared over the hill just as Screech hopped down from his tree house. He stretched his arms high into the air and yawned. "What a wonderful day," he said to no one in particular. He looked down and saw the coconut Shadow had left.

"Breakfast!" He smiled. He picked up the coconut, broke it over a rock, and drank the smooth coconut milk. It was delicious.

When he finished drinking, Screech noticed the arrow in the dirt. It pointed to a spot three trees away. He scratched his head and grinned.

"Does he really think I'm going to fall for this?" the monkey said to a passing butterfly. He closed his eyes and thought back to some of Shadow's other pranks.

There was the trick with the swamp water pineapples. How horrible they had tasted.

Then was the stunt with the hidden beehive. It took him weeks to get that sticky honey off his fur! Why did he keep falling for Shadow's stupid tricks?

Screech shrugged and followed the arrow.

Dreamer the rhinoceros and Ponder the frog stood well behind Honk the camel as he bent over his cluttered work table. Both Dreamer and Ponder had seen strange things happen when Honk was inventing.

"There, that should do it!" the camel said as he handed the rhino a very large donut-shaped object. It was made from soft leaves and branches. Dreamer turned it over and over, put it on his head and then tried to take a bite of it.

"It's not something to wear or eat!" Honk sputtered. "Just sit on it instead of the ground. You'll be fine in a few days. And next time don't stop right in front of the flinger when I'm about to test it," reminded Honk. "Couldn't you use something besides those sharp sticks to see if it works? That hurt!" Dreamer frowned as he rubbed his bottom.

As Dreamer tried Honk's new invention,
Screech rushed up to the three.
He carried four coconuts.

"I've been following his clues all
morning, but I haven't found anything
except a lot of coconuts. I'm getting
very tired of carrying coconuts and
very full from drinking coconut milk.
I'm getting very tired of this coconut caper!"

Honk, Dreamer, and Ponder
exchanged glances. What was Screech
talking about?

"Why do you think Shadow
is playing a trick on you, Screech?"
asked Ponder.

"Oh, he's just trying to
get even for a trick I played
on him last week," explained
the green monkey.
"I had him convinced
that Dreamer was going
to paint him purple
and tell Ivory he
was a grape."

"No wonder Shadow ran away from me every time I said hello," said Dreamer.

"That explains why Shadow kept giving Ivory all those blueberries, too," added Honk.

"Have you ever heard of the Golden Rule, Screech?" asked Ponder.

"Does it have something to do with the treasure Stretch was hunting for?"

"No, no. The Golden Rule says, 'Do to others as you would have them do to you,'" Ponder told him.

"What does that mean?"

"It means that if you want to stop Shadow from playing tricks on you, you have to stop playing tricks on him, too. Treat Shadow the way you want him to treat you!"

"Oh. Well that's no fun," Screech mumbled as he swung away.

Deep in the forest, Screech stared at another coconut. He carefully poked it with a stick as if the coconut or something under it were going to explode. Nothing happened. He looked under the coconut and saw still another arrow. "I'm not going to play this game anymore!" He grabbed the coconut and tramped away in the direction of the arrow.

In the meantime,
Shadow was placing still
more coconut and arrow clues.
He put one in Cozy Cave, another
under the waterfall, another
in the shallow waters of the pond,
and a final coconut on the beach.
Ponder, Howler the lion, Stretch the giraffe,
and Flutter the dove watched his antics.

Finally Ponder could not stand it any longer.
"Shadow," he called to the raccoon,
"what in the world are you doing?
I cannot believe that you want to
be this mean to your friend Screech.
Now what is this about?"
Shadow stopped his scampering for a moment.
"I can't tell you anything yet. You'll know soon.
Right now it is my secret."
Ponder told Shadow about the Golden Rule.
"Is this how you would have Screech treat you?" he asked.
Shadow looked at the frog and then at the others.
He seemed to be deciding something.
Finally, the raccoon nodded and signaled
for all the animals to gather around him.
He stood in the middle and told them
his secret. When he had finished,
Ponder and all the others laughed.
"That is a wonderful trick, Shadow!"
Ponder said.

An exhausted Screech stumbled out of the forest carrying eight coconuts. He followed the final clues that had led him in a circle to Cozy Cave, the waterfall, and the shallow waters of the pond. At each location he took the coconut. Finally, he followed the last arrow to the coconut on the beach. Wearily, he threw the eleven coconuts onto the sand and sat down beside them. He leaned over and rolled the last coconut away. Under this coconut was a large "X."

"Now what does this mean?" Screech sighed. "Maybe I am ready for the Golden Rule."

Slowly, from hiding spots near the beach, the other animals gathered around the tired monkey. Screech looked from one animal to another. When his gaze found Shadow, the monkey jumped to his feet. "Okay, I know this was your trick, but I don't understand any of it. Why the coconuts? Why the arrows? What's the point?"

"Well, Screech, the reason for the coconuts was so that we would all have something to eat. The reason for the arrows was to get you to this very spot at this very time. And the point of the trick was to say this:

HAPPY BIRTHDAY, SCREECH!

With that, the raccoon threw his arms around his friend and hugged him. Then all the other animals joined in. It was the very first birthday party in Noah's Park. It would certainly not be the last.

Later, as the sun set over the park, Ponder sat watching Shadow and Screech play on the beach. He smiled. "Well, God, this was certainly an exciting day. We began a Noah's Park tradition of celebrating a birthday with a great party. Maybe we also started a tradition of treating each other a little better, too. I like that idea even more than the parties." Ponder thought for a moment...

"Then again, next month is my birthday..."

The End.

DREAMER HAS A NIGHTMARE

Dreamer the rhinoceros loves to dream, until one day he has his first nightmare. How will Dreamer handle this frightening experience? Discover the answer in the Noah's Park adventure, Dreamer Has a Nightmare.

STRETCH'S TREASURE HUNT

Stretch the giraffe grew up watching her parents search for the Treasure of Nosy Rock. Imagine what happens when she finds out that the treasure might be buried in Noah's Park. Watch the fur fly as Stretch and her friends look for treasure in Stretch's Treasure Hunt.

CAMELS DON'T FLY

Honk the camel finds a statue of a camel with wings. Now, he is convinced that he can fly, too. Will Honk be the first camel to fly? Find out in the Noah's Park adventure, Camels Don't Fly.

HONK'S BIG ADVENTURE

On the first day of spring, all the animals of Noah's Park are playing in the mud, water, and leaves. This good clean fun creates a lot of dirty animals. When Honk the camel sees the mess, he decides to leave Noah's Park and find a clean place to live. Will Honk find what he searches for? Find out in the hilarious Noah's Park story, Honk's Big Adventure.

PONDER MEETS THE POLKA DOTS

Ponder the frog is growing lily pads in the Noah's Park pond. When something starts eating the lily pads, the normally calm frog decides to get even. Will Ponder save his lily pads? Find out in the colorful Noah's Park adventure, Ponder Meets the Polka Dots.